ギターのための

ムソルグスキー／編曲●山下和仁
# 展覧会の絵

Modest Petrovich Mussorgsky : Pictures at an Exhibition for guitar

Arranged for guitar by Kazuhito Yamashita

YAMASHITA EDITION　Vol.1

株式会社 現代ギター社
GG585
GENDAI GUITAR CO., LTD.
1-16-14 Chihaya, Toshima-ku, Tokyo, Japan

### ●山下和仁プロフィール

1961年長崎市に生まれ、父、山下亨に8歳よりギターを学ぶ。また作曲家の小船幸次郎に師事。

15歳で全国コンクール（現：東京国際ギターコンクール）に優勝のあと、1977年、16歳の時にラミレス、アレッサンドリア国際、パリ国際の世界三大ギターコンクールに、いずれも史上最年少優勝という快挙を成し遂げた。

LP、CD 合わせてこれまでに78枚のアルバムを発表。1980年発表の自身の編曲による〈展覧会の絵〉が大反響を得る。以後、〈火の鳥〉〈シェエラザート〉〈新世界より〉などオーケストラ曲用大曲をギター用に次々アレンジ、さらに「J.S.バッハ：無伴奏ヴァイオリンソナタ＆パルティータ、チェロ、フルート、リュート組曲 BWV995-1013（5CDs）」を全て編曲。かたわら「F. ソル：ギター曲全集（16CDs）」「H. ヴィラ＝ロボス：12の練習曲と5つのエチュード」「M. カステルヌオーヴォ＝テデスコ：ゴヤによる24のカプリチョス」など、ギター本来のレパートリーも名演の誉れ高く、広大なレパートリーを有する。

ウイーン・ムジークフェライン大ホール、ニューヨーク・リンカーンセンターほか世界各地でソロリサイタル。L. スラトキン、R. フリューベック・デ・ブルゴスなど世界的指揮者やオーケストラとも数々共演。また、ジャズ・ギタリストのラリー・コリエル、フルートの J. ゴールウェイ、コントラバスのゲリー・カー、東京クヮルテットなどと共演。2004年からは自身の子供たちと「山下和仁ファミリーカルテット・クインテット」を結成し、長女（紅弓）、次女（愛陽）ともギターデュオを組み、世界各地で公演。

国内外の作曲家、特にアジアの作曲家たちの新作委嘱初演にも意欲的で、山下和仁のために書かれた作品は60曲を越えている。CD『黎明期の日本ギター曲集』で平成11年度文化庁芸術祭大賞を受賞。

### ● Kazuhito Yamashita

Born in Nagasaki in 1961, Kazuhito Yamashita began studying the guitar at age 8 and under the continuing supervision of his father Toru and also the composer Kojiro Kobune.

He won the Tokyo International Guitar Competition (1976) at the age of 15 years and consecutively won historic laurels as the youngest winner, at 16, in the world's top competitions (1977), the Ramirez Guitar Concours (Spain), the Alessandria Guitar Competition (Italy), the Paris International Guitar Competition.

He has released 78 titles, CD and LP. In 1980, Yamashita launched, to critical acclaim and worldwide sales, his landmark arrangement of 'Pictures at an Exhibition'. This was rapidly followed a several orchestral pieces arranged for the guitar and attracting considerable attention, such as 'Firebird' and 'Scheherazade' and, more recently, the 'New World Symphony' (Symphony No.9 from the New World). In addition, he released an acclaimed collection of guitar pieces including 5 CDs of the J.S Bach sonatas and partitas for violin, cello, lute and flute (BWV 995-1013), transcribed for the guitar by himself, as well as essential works for the guitar such as 16 CDs of the complete Fernando Sor and works by H. Villa-Lobos: 5 Preludes and 12 Etudes as well as M. Castelnuovo-Tedesco's '24 Caprichos de Goya'.

His worldwide appearances include recitals at the Vienna Musikverein 'Great Hall' and New York's Lincoln Center. He has collaborated under such eminent conductors such as Leonard Slatkin and Rafael Frühbeck de Burgos, and with numerous performers such as jazz guitarist Larry Coryell, James Galway (flute), Gary Karr (double bass) and the Tokyo String Quartet. From 2004, there were new directions with his children, in the 'Yamashita Family Guitar Quartet/Quintet,' and duos, performed worldwide, with his daughters Koyumi and Kanahi.

Yamashita is an enthusiastic proponent of new works for the guitar and has given the world premier of over 60 new compositions from both Japan and overseas. In 1999, he received the National Arts Festival Grand Prize from the Japanese Government's Agency for Cultural Affairs for his CD recording of Japanese Guitar Music 1923-1948.

*English Translation. John C. Maher*

### ● 作品データ

* 1980年7月13日　長崎ギター音楽院第108回サロン・コンサートにて初演。
* 1980年10月より、東京文化会館小ホール（'80年10月15日）、アムステルダム・コンセルトヘボウ小ホール（11月14日）、長崎市民会館（11月23日）、トロント、ソウル（'84年）、台北、ロンドン、メットマン、ウィーン（'85年）他、各地のリサイタルで発表。
* 1981年3月10日～11日、入間市民会館にてレコーディング、'81年6月21日、楽譜と同時に発売（RCL-8042）。'82年1月アメリカ盤（ARC 1-4203）、6月ヨーロッパ盤（RL-14203）発売。'83年、ドイツ・レコード賞受賞。

（1981年初版時のものを再掲）

### ● Works

- 13 July 1980. Nagasaki Guitar Ongakuin's 108th Salon Concert. Debut Performance.
- October 1980- Tokyo Bunka Kaikan Recital Hall (15.10.'80), Amsterdam Concertgebouw Recital Hall (14.11.'80), Nagasaki Shimin Kaikan (11.23.'80), Toronto, Seoul (1984), Taipei, London, Vienna (1985), other locations to be announced.
- March 10-11 1981. Iruma Shimin Kaikan, recording. 21 June 1981, release of disk (RCL-8042) and publication of sheet music. 1982, January, US release (ARC 1-4203) and June, European release (RL-14293), 1983, Deutsche Grammophon Grand Prix.

(Reused from 1st edition in 1981)

## ●序

　ギターは素晴らしい楽器です。そこに秘められた表現力の可能性は、測りしれません。私は、この豊かな楽器とともに生きていることを大変幸福に思います。そして、この楽器を手に音楽を創造することに情熱を持っています。

　ギターの凄さについては、ずいぶん昔から言われていますが、今世紀になって登場した巨匠アンドレス・セゴビアをはじめとする偉大なるアーティスト達によって急速に証明され、さらにその世界を広げています。すなわち、ギターで演奏される音楽はルネッサンスから現代に及ぶようになり、独奏のみならず、協奏曲、室内楽、重奏、伴奏、合奏などの世界でも少しずつギターの存在価値が生まれています。また、少ないレパートリーの問題も、現代の作曲家の作品、および、優れた編曲により、しだいに解決され演奏芸術の可能性も大きくなっています。さらに、作品内容も小品ばかりでなく大曲の出現が現実となっています。そして、ギターはクラシック音楽の世界でも重要な位置を占めつつあると思われます。

　このような中で、私は小さい頃より、ギターで今よりさらにスケールの大きい表現ができるのではないかと思い常日頃追及してきました。つまり、もっとダイナミック、シンフォニックなどの表現方法を用い、さらに現代感覚に富んだ演奏ができないものか、そして独奏楽器として最も表現力豊かなギターによって、もっと長大な大曲を演奏できないものか、その他いろいろと試みてきました。そして以上のようなことにより、さらに芸術の本質に迫る音楽を創造したいと強く思ってきました。

　このような考えの中から今回の発想が生まれてきました。それは、ロシアの大作曲家モデスト・ペトローヴィチ・ムソルグスキーの代表的ピアノ曲である組曲《展覧会の絵》全曲を、世界で初めてギターで弾くということです。

　一昨年の春に思いつき、このために自ら本格的編曲に初挑戦することを決意し、限りない努力をしてきました。そして、この極めて魅力ある曲によって、小さい頃からの課題とさらに取り組んだわけです。もちろんその際、未熟者なるがために、途中でずいぶんさまざまな場面に遭遇し、とても文章にはならないさまざまな思いや経験をしました。

　本格的発表の決断は、かなりむずかしく、最も身近な師である父と、作曲家で指揮者でもあられる小船幸次郎先生に貴重なアドバイスをいただきました。その後、関係者の皆様の御助力により、多数のリサイタル、レコーディング、そしてさらに今回は私にとって初めての出版が実現できました。心から感謝しています。

1981年6月　山下和仁
（1981年初版序文を再掲）

## ● Author's Comment

The guitar is a superlative instrument, concealing the incalculable potential of expressive power. I am happy to have been given the opportunity to share its company and enrich my own life. This instrument can be instilled, in one's grasp, with the emotion of musical creation.

We have been told of the wonder of the guitar from long ago. In our era, this has been confirmed with the appearance of the maestro Andre Segovia and the rapid emergence of other important figures in the expanding world of the guitar. In the present day, music for the guitar spans Renaissance to modern and its value is now recognized not only in solo work but concerto, chamber music, duo, in the role of accompaniment and ensemble. The problem of a paucity of contemporary music for the guitar, is gradually being addressed by an emerging number of pieces by contemporary composers and outstanding arrangements of older pieces expanding the potential for performance. In addition, larger works as well as small pieces are now emerging. The guitar is, indeed, I am convinced, becoming a fundamental part of the world of classical music.

In this respect, I have long been convinced, from an early age to the present, of the guitar's even greater expressive potential. That is to say, I have endeavoured to view the instrument as a means of dynamic and symphonic expressiveness, a contemporary sensibility and offering also, as a solo instrument, unparalleled richness. All this leads me to the inescapable conviction that such music approaches the very essence of art and a strong desire to be part of its creation.

Thus, from these thoughts emerges such a conception and led me to the great Russian composer M. P. Mussorgsky's signature work the piano suite 'Pictures at an Exhibition' and to play the entire piece, a world first, on the guitar.

The idea occurred to me two years ago, in spring, and I decided to embark seriously on my first challenge; a piece arranged by myself and I made strenuous effort. It was an extremely attractive piece of music and it made me commit further to the lifelong task of arrangement. Needless to say, being an immature arranger, I stumbled in the process; many different experiences I cannot put into words. Also, the decision to go public with this piece was not easy. I consulted my teacher (father) and the composer-conductor Kojiro Kobune. From them I received invaluable advice. Other people helped on the road to publication. Finally, it was done. From that point, I was able to accomplish many recitals and recordings and then came my first publication of sheet music. I am truly grateful.

1981, June.
Kazuhito Yamashita
(Reused from 1st edition in 1981)

*English Translation. John C. Maher*

# Pictures at an Exhibition | Table
## 展覧会の絵 | 目次

    Promenade —— 6
    プロムナード

I   Gnomus —— 7
    こびと

    Promenade —— 11
    プロムナード

II  Il vecchio castello —— 12
    古城

    Promenade —— 15
    プロムナード

III  The Tuileries —— 16
    チュイルリーの庭

IV  Bydlo —— 18
    ビドロ

    Promenade —— 20
    プロムナード

V  Ballet of the Little Chickens —— 21
    卵のからをつけたひなの踊り

VI  Samuel Goldenberg und Schmuyle —— 24
    サミュエル・ゴールデンベルクとシュミュイレ

VII  A Market Place in Limoges —— 26
    リモージュの市場

VIII  Catacombae (Sepulcrum romanum, Con mortuis in lingua mortua) —— 30
    カタコンブ

IX  The Hut of Baba-Yaga —— 32
    バーバ・ヤーガの小屋

X  The Bohatyr Gate of Kiev —— 40
    キエフの大門

    Explanation for Performance —— 46
    奏法解説

# PICTURES AT AN EXHIBITION
展覧会の絵

## Promenade
プロムナード

Modest Petrovich Mussorgsky (1874)
Arranged for Guitar by
Kazuhito Yamashita (1980)

Allegro giusto, nel modo russico,
senza allegrezza, ma poco sostenuto

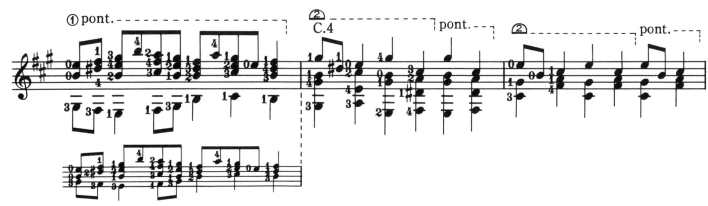

## I Gnomus
こびと

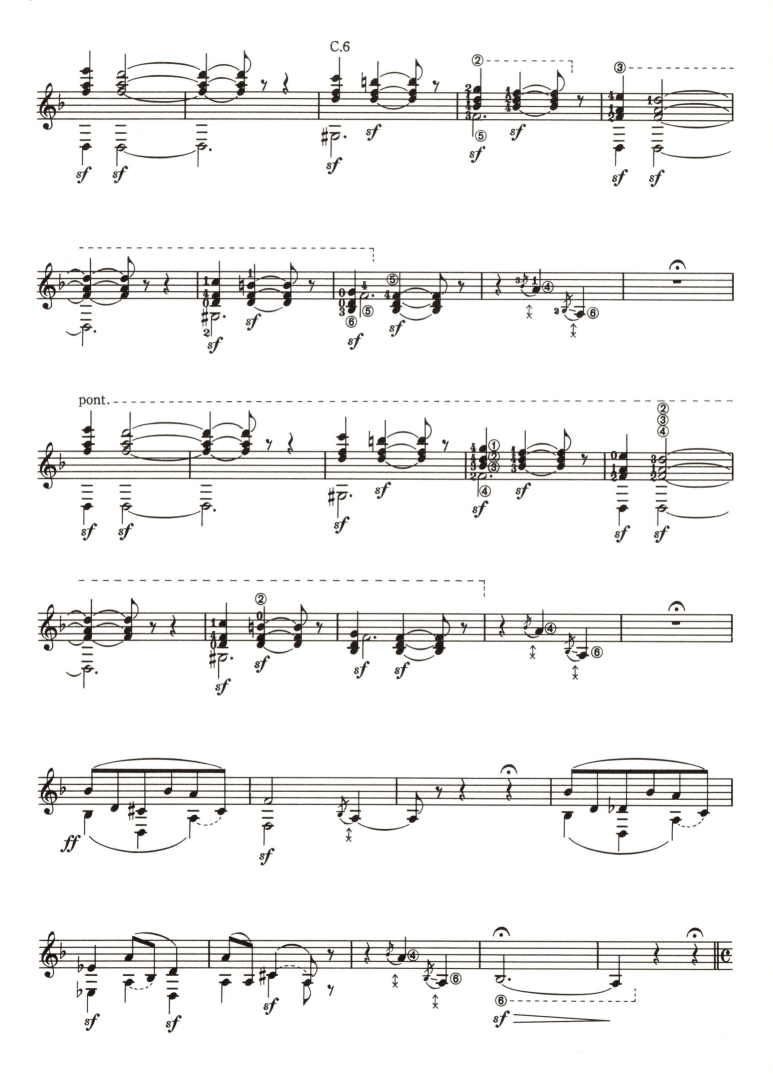

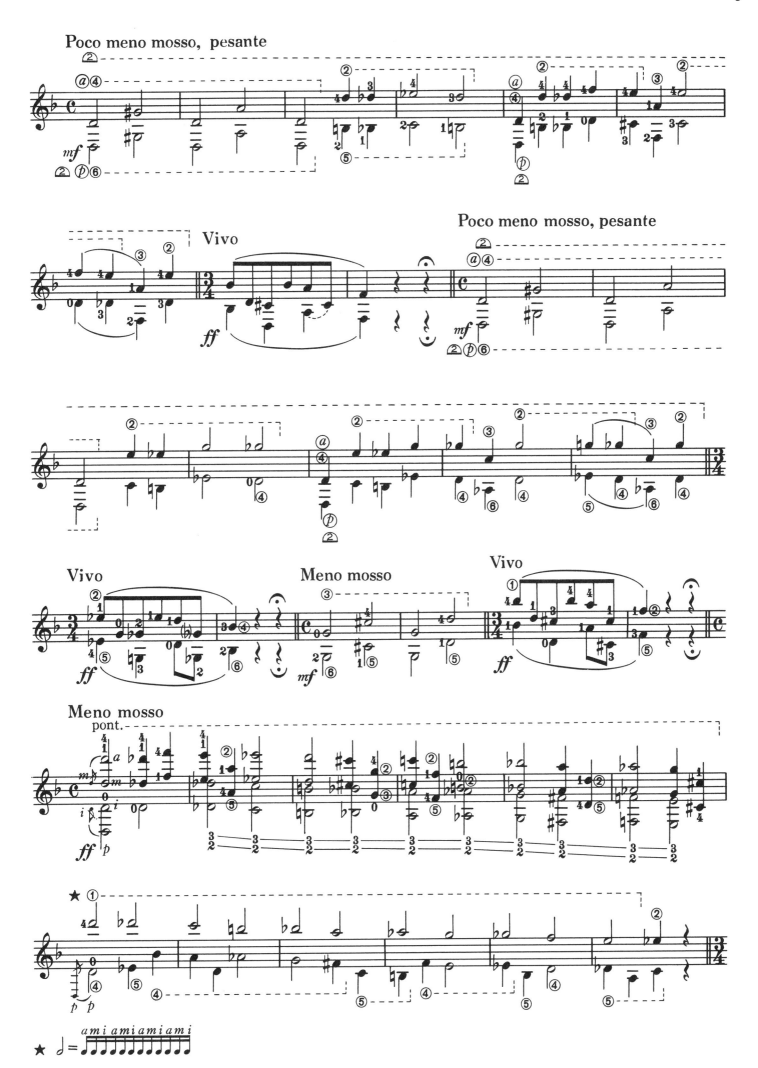

# Promenade
プロムナード

attacca

# II Il vecchio castello
古城

⑤=G
⑥=D

Andantino molto cantabile e con dolore

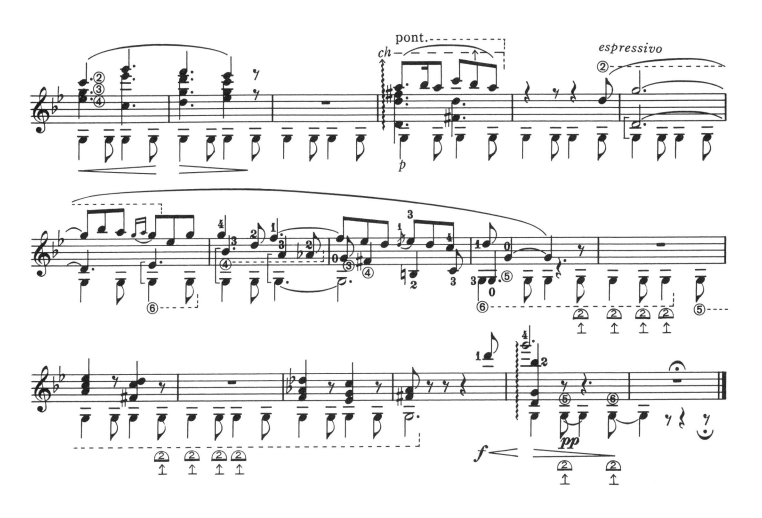

## Promenade

プロムナード

⑤=G
⑥=D

Moderato non tanto, pesamente

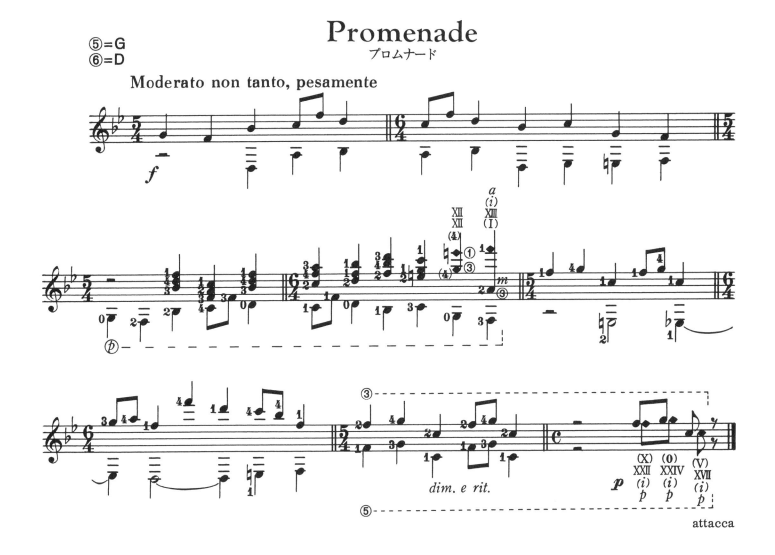

attacca

# III The Tuileries
チュイルリーの庭

# IV Bydlo

# Promenade
プロムナード

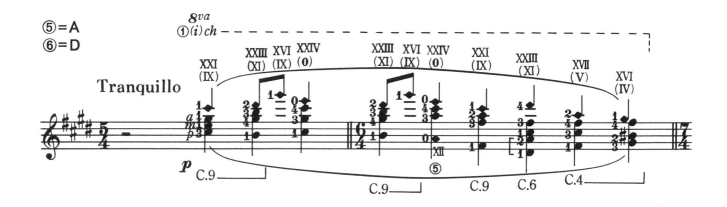

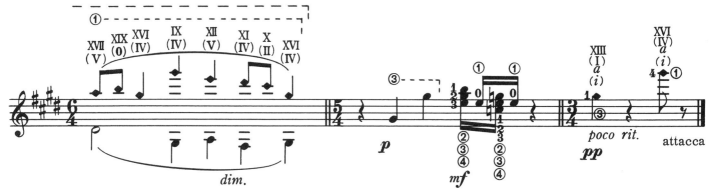

# V Ballet of the Little Chickens

卵のからをつけたひなの踊り

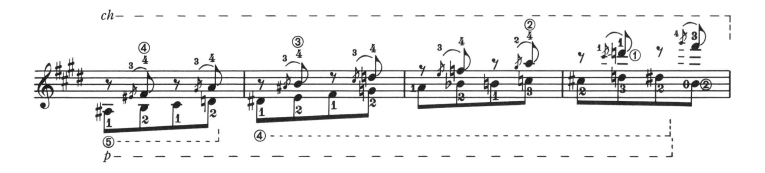

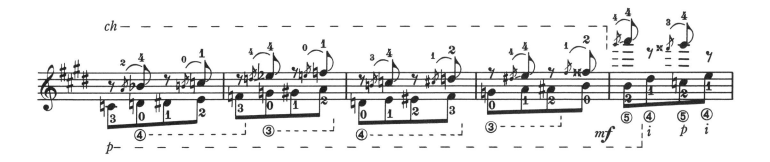
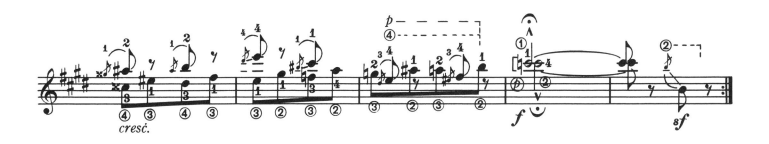

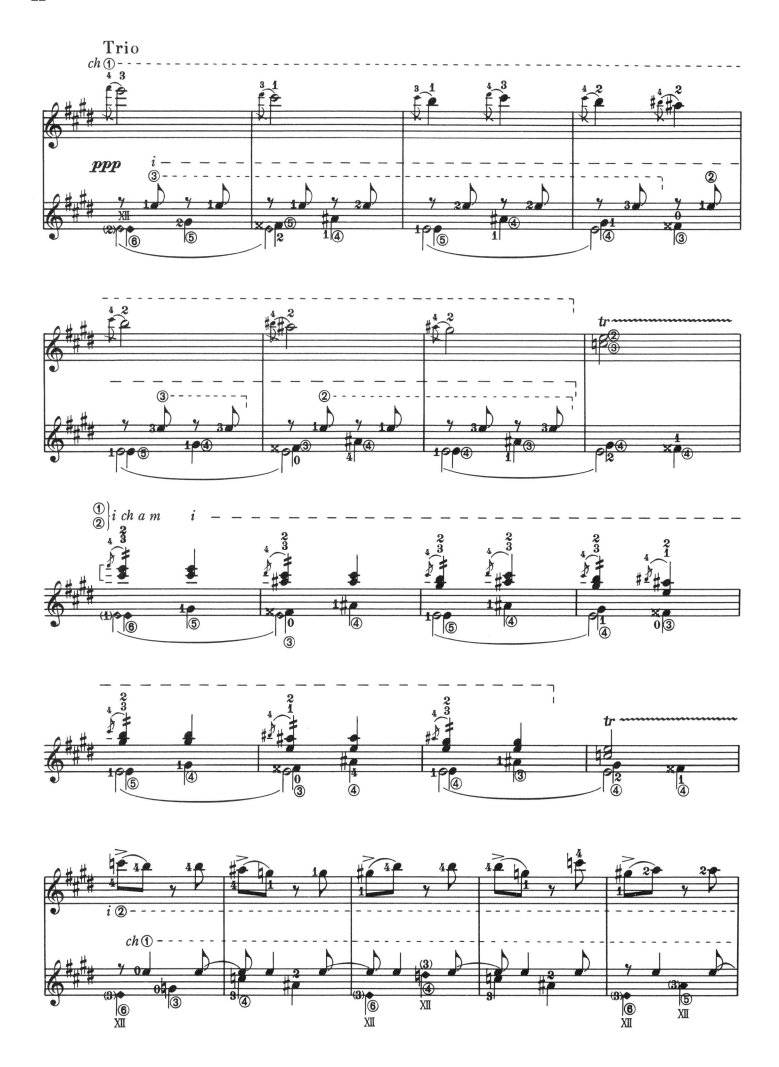

# VII A Market Place in Limoges

リモージュの市場

# VIII Catacombae
### カタコンブ
## Sepulcrum romanum

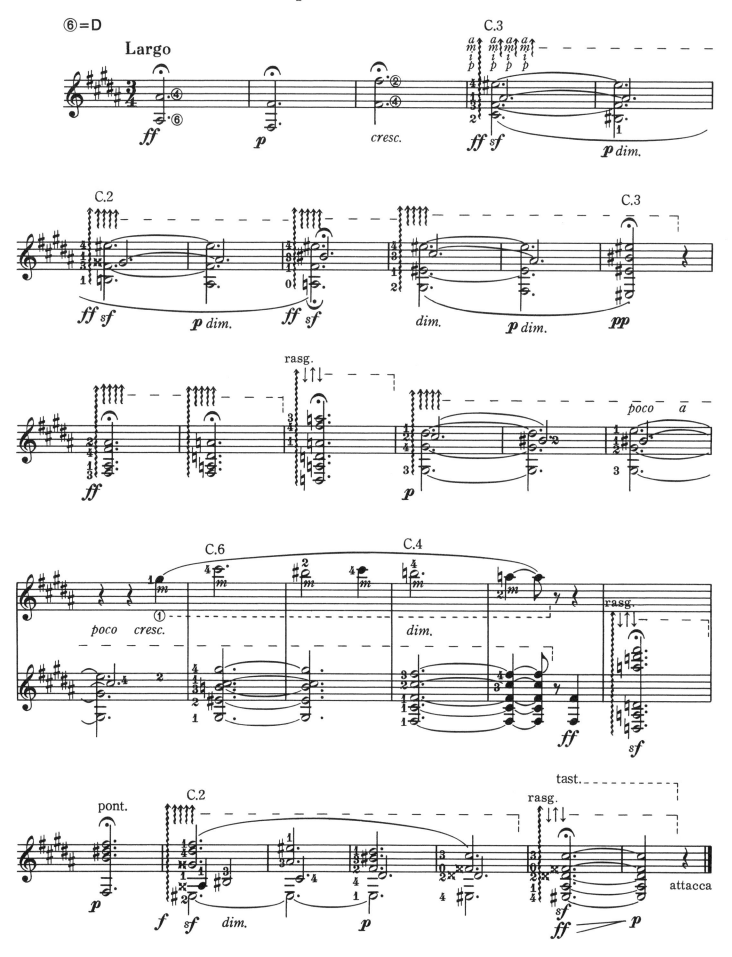

# Cum mortuis in lingua mortua

Andante non troppo, con lamento

# IX The Hut of Baba-Yaga

バーバ・ヤーガの小屋

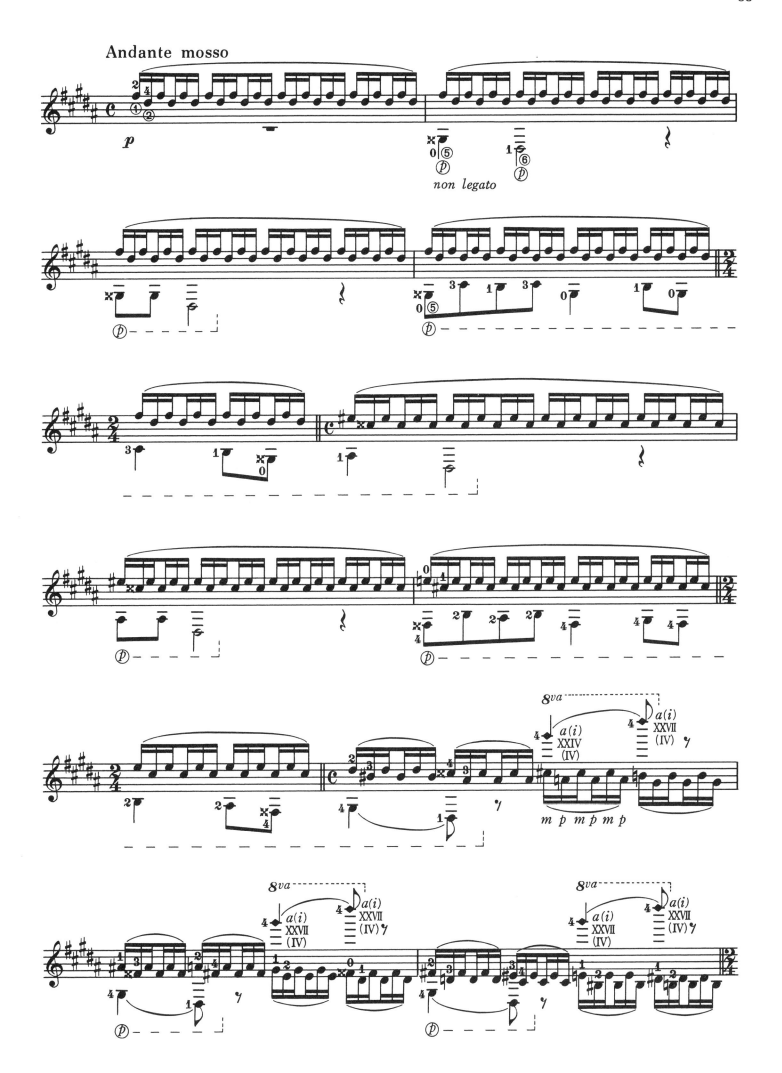

**Allegro molto**

# X The Bohatyr Gate of Kiev

キエフの大門

⑥=D

Allegro alla breve. Maestoso, Con grandezza

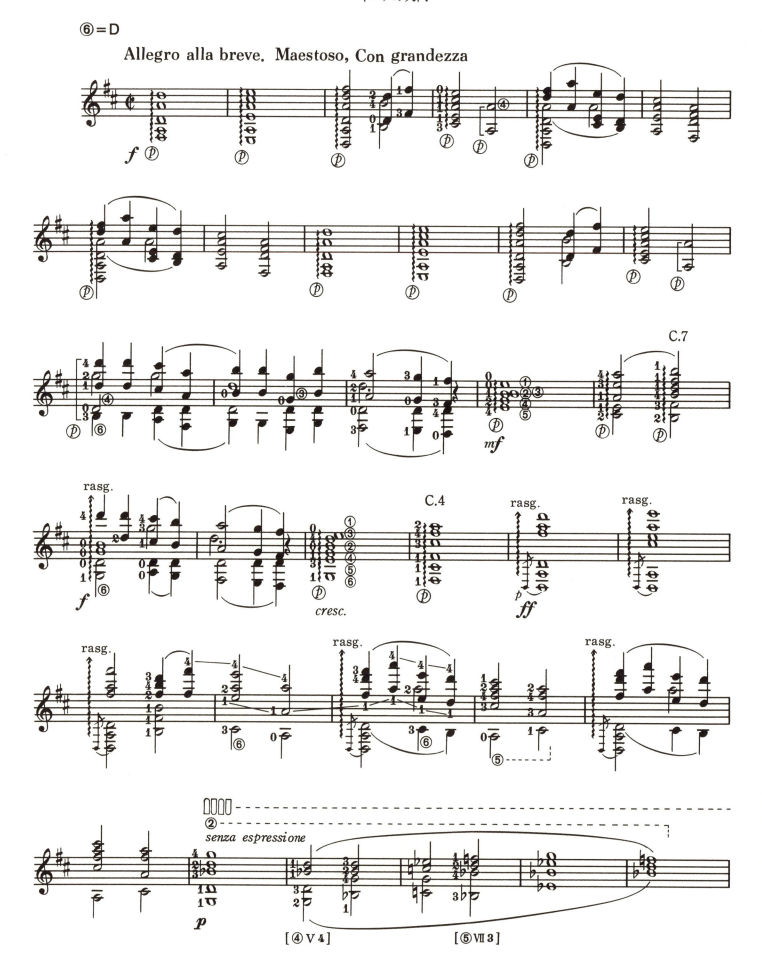

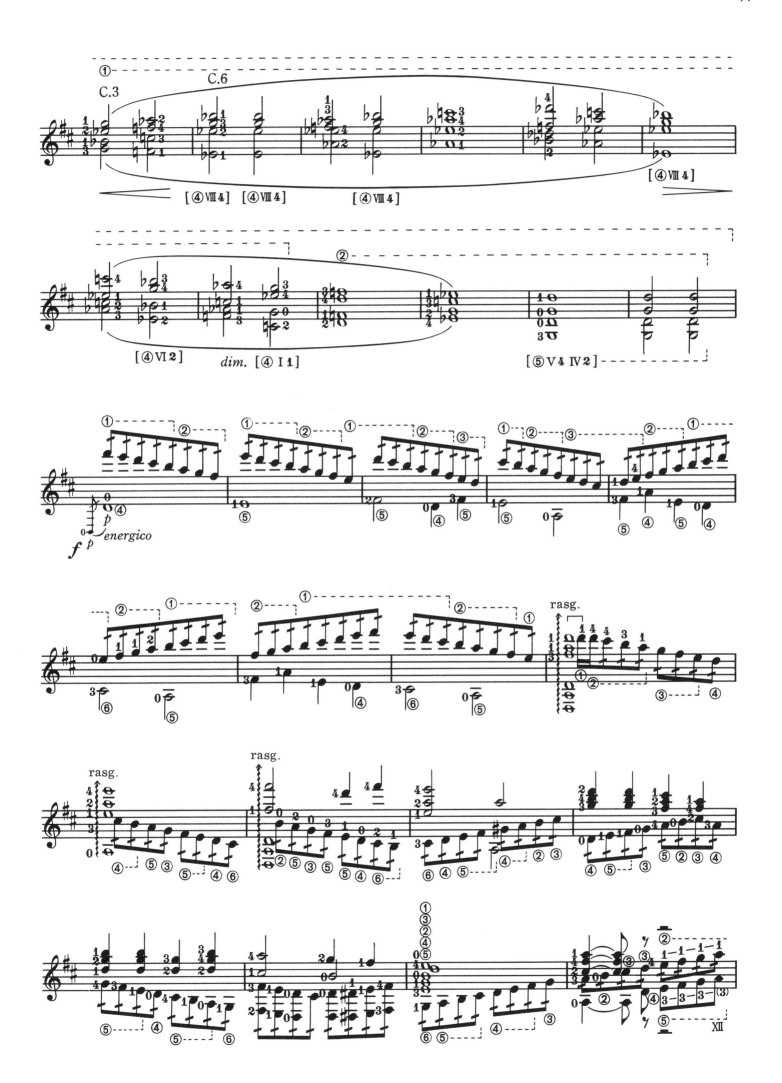

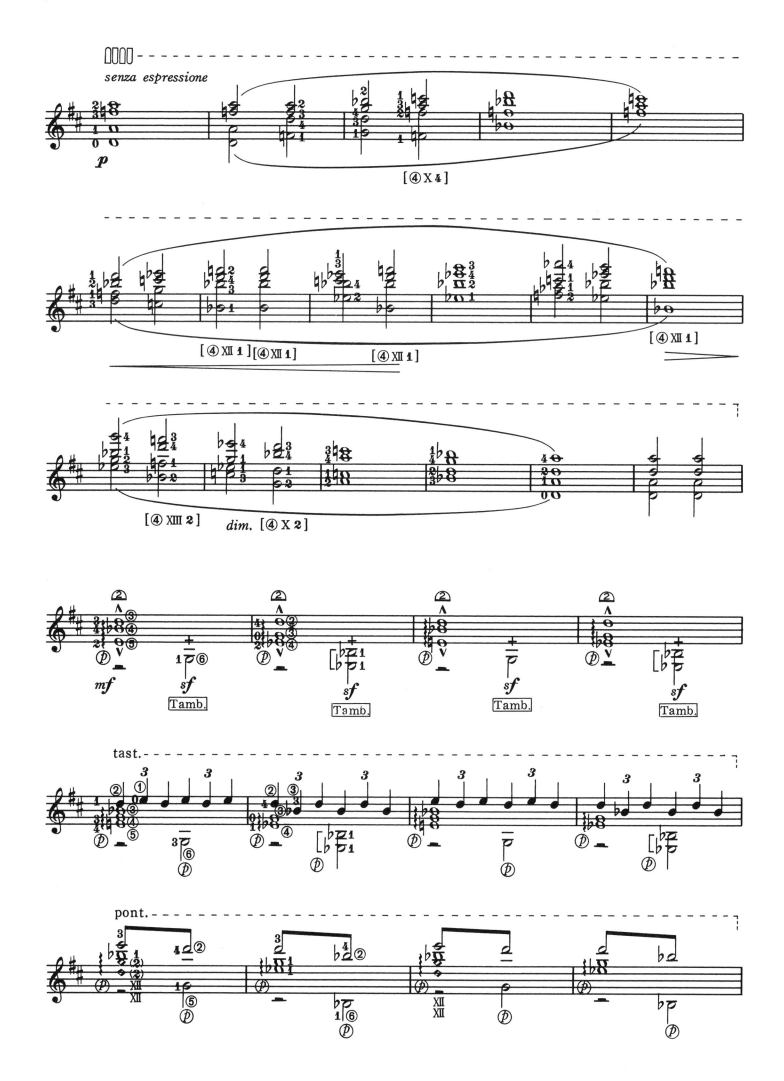

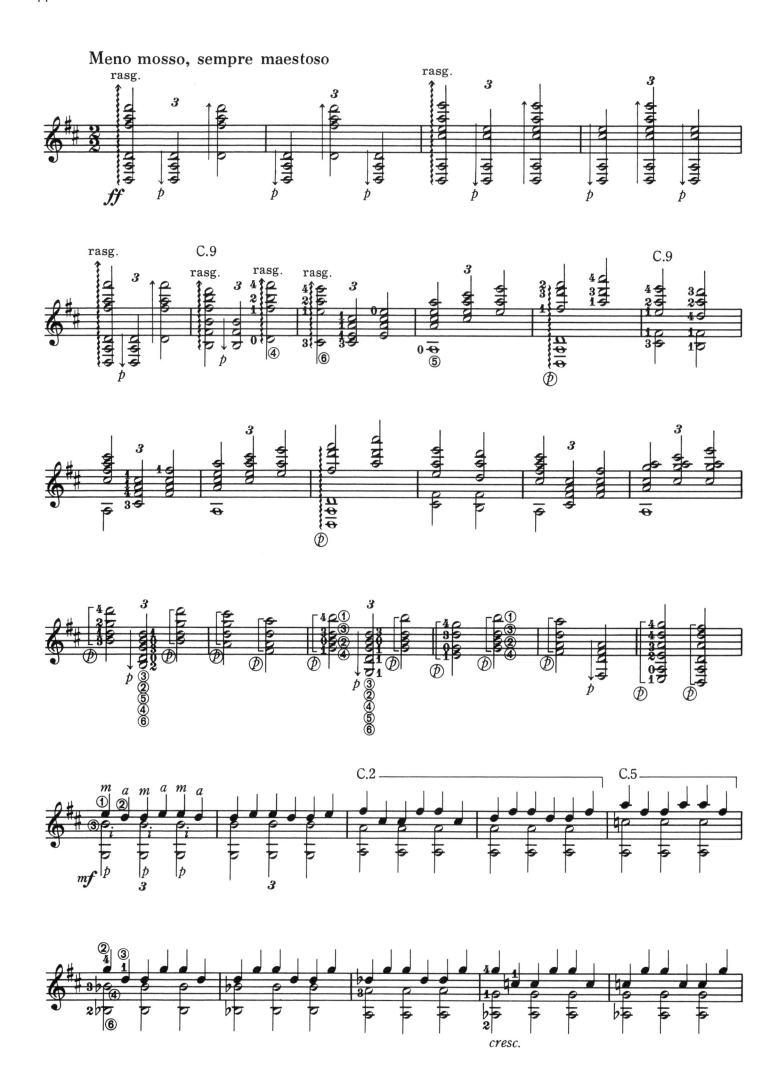

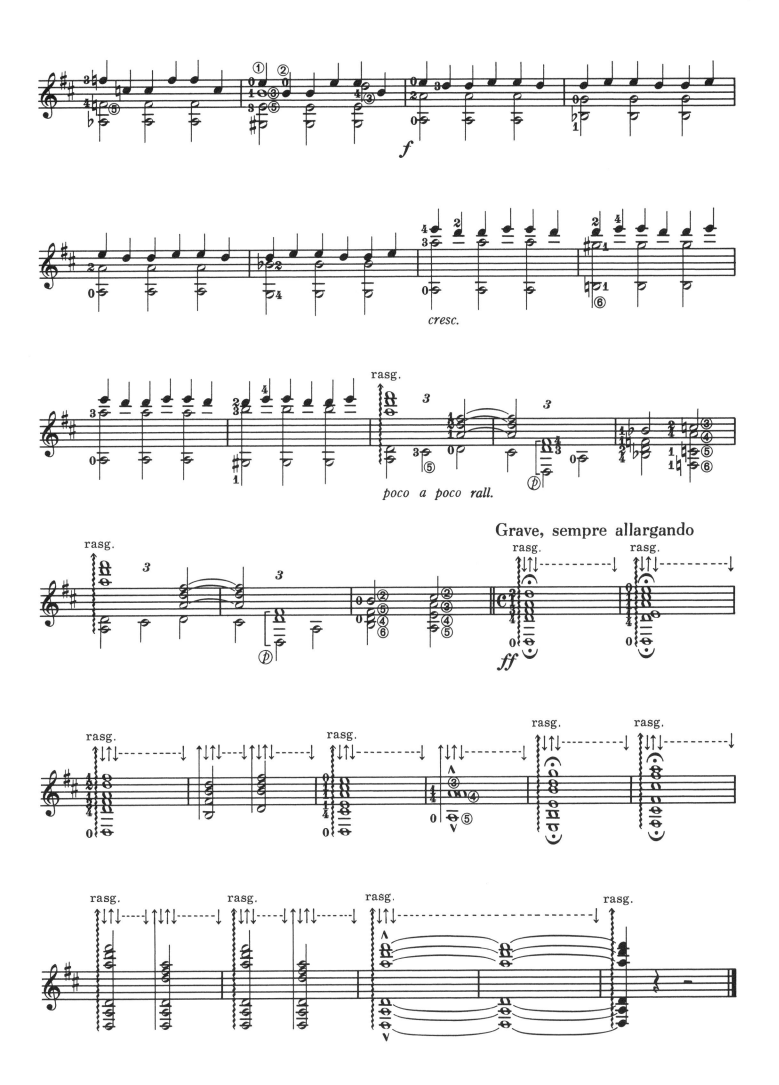

## ●奏法解説

ハーモニックス(♩ ♪など)……すべて実音で記譜
- 自然倍音
  - …… Ⅲ Ⅳ Ⅴ ……………ポジション
  - ( 1 2 3 4 )………触れる指
  - ①②③④⑤⑥……………弦
- 人工倍音
  - (… Ⅲ Ⅳ Ⅴ …)………左指の押えるポジション
  - ⅩⅤ ⅩⅥ ⅩⅦ ………右指の触れるポジション
  - 1 2 3 4 ……………押える指
  - (i) ………触れる指
  - p  a  ch ……………奏する指

*ch* ………chico，右手小指のこと

ⓟ ⓐ ……指頭奏法（爪は使わない）

↑ ↕ ……ⓟとⓐで弦をつまみ，表面板に対し垂直上向に奏す
- ↑ ……右指をはなした後，弦を指板に当てない場合
- ↕ ……右指をはなした後，弦を指板に当てる場合（バルトーク・ピチカートのようなもの）

[Tamb.] ……Tambora　タンボーラ
- ＋ ………ⓟによる
- × ………ⓜまたはⓐによる

⌢‿ ……技術的なスラー

𝄀𝄀𝄀𝄀 ……*pima pima* による急速なアルペジオを音符の長さ続ける

tremolo
↑↓↑↓ ……指定された指（*i* または *ch*）の爪によるトレモロ（マンドリンにおけるピックの役割を爪に与える）

↑↓↑↓ ……和音のトレモロ

𝄀𝄀𝄀𝄀 ……ⓘⓜⓐなどによる和音のトレモロ（爪は使わない）
〔　〕は間の不用弦の処理方法を示す
- ④ ⑤ ……弦
- … Ⅴ Ⅵ ……触れるポジション（押えない）
- 1 2 3 4 ……触れる指（押えない）

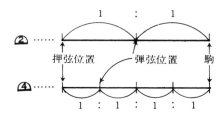

rasg.
↕ ………graneado　グラネアード

↑ ………rasgueado seco　ラスゲアード・セコ

〔 ………指定された指だけによる重音奏法

## ● EXPLANATION FOR PERFORMANCE

Harmonics(♩ ♪ etc.)…………all notated in actual notes.
- Natural harmonics.
  - … Ⅲ Ⅳ Ⅴ ………position
  - ( 1 2 3 4 )………Fingering
  - ①②③④⑤⑥………String
- Artificial harmonics
  - (… Ⅲ Ⅳ Ⅴ …) ………position to be held by left finger.
  - ⅩⅤ ⅩⅥ ⅩⅦ ……Position to be touched by right finger.
  - 1 2 3 4 ………Finger to hold.
  - (i) …………Finger to touch.
  - p  a  ch ………Finger to play.

*ch* ………chico, Little finger of the right hand.

ⓟ ⓐ ……Play with fingertips (nails are not used).

↑ ↕ ……Pluck the string with ⓟ and ⓐ and play upwards and vertically against the sound board.
- ↑ ……After letting right fingers go, do not hit the string against fret board
- ↕ ……After letting right fingers go, hit the string against fret board

[Tamb.] ……Tambora.
- ＋ ………with ⓟ
- × ………with ⓜ or ⓐ

⌢‿ ……Left hand slur.

𝄀𝄀𝄀𝄀 ……Continue to play rapid arpegio by *pima pima* …… for the length of the note.

tremolo
↑↓↑↓ ……Tremolo with the nails of indicated finger (*i* or *ch*). (This gives the nails the role of mandolin pick).

↑↓↑↓ ……Tremolo in chord.

𝄀𝄀𝄀𝄀 ……Tremolo in chord by ⓘ ⓜ or ⓐ (nails are not used).
[ ] indicates the manner of treating unused strings in between played strings.
- ④ ⑤ ……String
- … Ⅴ Ⅵ ……Position to touch (Do not hold).
- 1 2 3 4 ……Finger to touch (Do not hold).

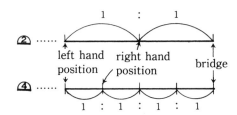

rasg.
↕ ………graneado.

↑ ………rasgueado seco.

〔 ………Double stopping played only by the indicated fingers.

## 山下和仁エディション・シリーズ復刊
『展覧会の絵』『新世界より』を始め、全世界に衝撃をもたらした、
山下和仁の歴史的名編曲が待望の完全復刻。順次刊行予定!!

[第1集] ムソルグスキー『展覧会の絵』(山下和仁 編曲)
菊倍判・48頁　定価[本体2,400円+税]【GG585】

[第2集] ドヴォルザーク『新世界より』全曲(山下和仁 編曲)
菊倍判・68頁　定価[本体2,600円+税]【GG590】

【以下続刊】

ドヴォルザーク『ラルゴ』/ヒメネス『アロンソの結婚』(山下和仁 編曲)
菊倍判・32頁

リスト『ハンガリー狂詩曲第2番』/サン=サーンス『白鳥』/パガニーニ『カプリス No.24』(山下和仁 編曲)
菊倍判・40頁

バッハ『無伴奏ヴァイオリンのためのソナタとパルティータ』(山下和仁 編曲)

　無伴奏ヴァイオリンのためのソナタ第1番 BWV1001
　　菊倍判・16頁

　無伴奏ヴァイオリンのためのパルティータ第1番 BWV1002
　　菊倍判・18頁

　無伴奏ヴァイオリンのためのソナタ第2番 BWV1003
　　菊倍判・20頁

　無伴奏ヴァイオリンのためのパルティータ第2番 BWV1004
　　菊倍判・32頁

　無伴奏ヴァイオリンのためのソナタ第3番 BWV1005
　　菊倍判・20頁

　無伴奏ヴァイオリンのためのパルティータ第3番 BWV1006
　　菊倍判・20頁

ドビュッシー『小組曲』/『パスピエ』(山下和仁 編曲)　※ギター二重奏
菊倍判・48頁

ベートーヴェン『ギター協奏曲』[原曲:ヴァイオリン協奏曲ニ長調 Op.61](山下和仁 編曲)　※ギターパートのみ
菊倍判・48頁

---

ギターのための
展覧会の絵
山下和仁 編曲
定価[本体2,400円+税]
GG585

Modest Petrovich Mussorgsky
Pictures at an Exhibition for guitar
Arranged for guitar by Kazuhito Yamashita

1981年6月30日初版発行　2016年8月20日新訂初版発行
発行元 ● 株式会社 現代ギター社
〒171-0044 東京都豊島区千早1-16-14
TEL03-3530-5423　FAX03-3530-5405
無断転載を禁ず
印刷・製本 ● シナノ印刷 株式会社
表紙 ● イトウコウヘイ
コード番号 ● ISBN 978-4-87471-585-7　C3373　¥2400E

© Gendai Guitar Co., Ltd.
1-16-14 Chihaya, Toshima-ku, Tokyo 171-0044, JAPAN
http://www.gendaiguitar.com
1st edition : June 30th, 1981　1st revision edition : August 20th, 2016
Printed in Japan

楽譜や歌詞・音楽書などの出版物を権利者に無断で複製(コピー)することは、著作権の侵害(私的利用など特別な場合を除く)にあたり、著作権法により罰せられます。
　また、出版物からの不法なコピーが行なわれますと、出版社は正常な出版活動が困難となり、ついには皆様方が必要とされるものも出版できなくなります。
　音楽出版社と日本音楽著作権協会(JASRAC)は、著作者の権利を守り、なおいっそう優れた作品の出版普及に全力をあげて努力してまいります。どうか不法コピーの防止に、皆様方のご協力をお願い申し上げます。

(株)現代ギター社
(社)日本音楽著作権協会